AF576650

between creatures
collected poems

for the child inside

May the divine light of the Supreme Being illuminate our intellect to lead us along a path of enlightenment.

(Gayatri Mantra)

collected poems

apocalypse

when the apocalypse comes,
at least you'll know how
to whittle us utensils
to eat your homemade granola
and drink your zangy kombucha.
i will have toe warmers
to keep our feet toasty for six hours;
hopefully enough time
to find a cat farm
where perhaps a llama or two reside.
we'll harvest hops and grapes,
and maybe a tomato will ripen.
and if you'll play your ukulele,
i'll smile broadly and sing off key.

you didn't realize i was magic

you didn't realize i was magic,
the way i can will things into existence
with a gentle touch and the right words.
i have a passion for every-day wonders,
and gratitude for each experience.

no, you said i was "too much."

but darling, you weren't enough.
you with your mood swings
and uncertainties because
that one time
you let yourself love someone
and it soured.

you didn't realize i was magic,
the way i cared for you tenderly
with the patience of a guru,
guiding you to find peace and growth.

you thanked me for helping you float.
but you could never throw me a rope back
because i anchored and buoyed you,
and – you – was all that mattered.

you didn't realize i was magic,
and when i asked if you were made of stardust,

it was just my own reflection
i saw in your eyes.

my own wisdom,
my own groundedness,
my own ability to love

you didn't realize i was magic
(and neither did i)

but i do now.

a woman round with love

they say time heals all wounds,
but let me tell you
not a day passes
that i don't think about my grandma.
the memories bloom within me,
sprouting from my bones.
i'm transported back to her home
filled with the smells of food
that fattened me up,
and the feeling of safety
that came radiating off
a woman round with love.

she taught me to play rummy
and i inherited my love of crosswords
and salty foods from her.
her perpetual smile
for strangers in grocery store parking lots
is part of my lineage.

they say time will heal it,
but not a day goes by that i don't have
the camera flash in my mind.

a memory:
she made me bring down her tomato plants
from upstairs to put on her porch,

and tie the akimbo stems to the railing
with old stockings.
every spring, this ritual.
and i'd pout because it cut into my time
of doing nothing.

a memory:
the summer she watched us
while our mother worked,
every day at 7 am we went to church.
yes.
every. day.
picture it — twenty old ladies wearing wrinkles
and pastel sweaters in eighty-degree heat,
their matching puffs of white hair
like halos atop their heads.
two little kids with pinched cheeks
praying for mass to pass quickly so that
we could go to swim practice.
then afterward, we shivered in towels
in the back seat of her tiny, old ford
while she stopped to buy a salami grinder
and have it cut in three so we could feast
during the price is right.

a memory:
sick on her couch,
she rubbed my back and
beat the bubbles out of ginger ale for me
and when i was well enough to eat,

i wanted her pot roast and creamy mashed potatoes,
that baked macaroni and cheese,
never from a box.

a memory:
she knew how to clench and unclench her first
to make the muscle in her arm jump.
she told me there was a mouse in there
running up and down.
i gazed at her wide-eyed with wonder, mouth agape,
and she laughed jiggling like jell-o
at the innocence of a child.

a memory:
her vivid death,
a massive heart attack.
i remember how fast her body went cold
how tight her teeth clenched,
yet
we tried to open them
to get her to breathe.
in the threshold between
the bathroom and the hallway,
in the threshold between
life and death,
my mom frantically pumps her mother's heart
just like every cpr lesson
you hope to never have to use.
my mom and i switch on and off,
fighting against my grandmother's mortality.

i can see the bloated tears,
streaming down my brother's cheeks
while he begs the 911 operator for help.

light years pass before the ambulance arrives
and the workers meander like sloths.
i want to scream my lungs off, but instead
i grab the ceramic cherub off her shelf
on the way to the hospital.
a totem i clutched in desperate desire
for a miracle.

but that didn't change things.

when we returned to her house,
the disbelief.

she can't be dead.

she didn't finish the water in her glass
or
today's solitaire game
or
her laundry
or
so many things.

i see that day so clearly,
but push it off because
...well,

why should this memory take precedence?

the memories:
so many commonplace experiences;
but like any good sage will tell you,
they are moments
simple and perfect.
they converge to create her legacy
of kindness and compassion.

i have a grandma-shaped hole in my heart,
round like she was,
and full of love.

my biggest regret

i hung my value
on the whim of your hook.

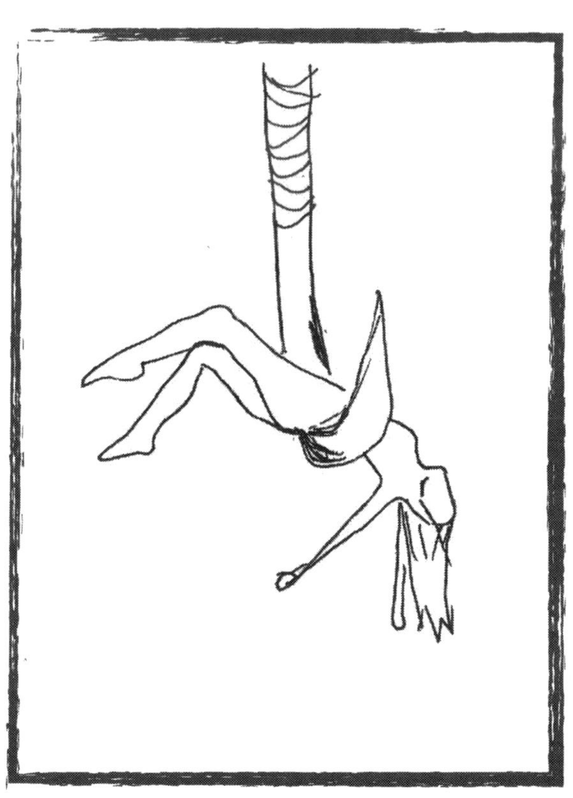

washed away

doctors should prescribe hot baths
to mend broken hearts,
wash away the tear stains
and relax the muscles of body and soul.
with my two kittens watching me
in the candlelight,
what else could compete?
makes me miss you a little less.
plus if i take a good cry,
my body can't tell the difference between
that and the epsom salt.
so i let it all go down the drain
push my thoughts away
enjoy the present moment,
which will be followed by the beauty
of some yoga and red wine.

i know that the end of every emotion
is silence.
the rippling of a pebble in a pond
or a lisa in a tub.
either way, the stillness brings comfort
not dread.

i am okay with myself.
i am okay without you.

ode to xavier*

today i found you
sunken
among the roots
and i shook frantic
the plant
hoping to wake you
from your dreams.

goodbye my blue friend.
maybe the angels
will remember to feed you.

* a beloved beta fish

a letter to the child inside

beautiful child;
may your spirit always feel
like she can fly,
that your dreams are the stuff
reality is made of,
that the world is full of possibilities
and the paths are abundant
and as exciting as fireworks.

beautiful child;
may you know emotions are natural
and expressing them takes courage.
finding the right words empowers you
and allows you a healthy way
to feel and renew and flourish.

beautiful child;
you have within you the entire universe.
you are made of moon beams and wishes.
you are filled with a soul as great as
any of the most brilliant artists and healers.
you have incredible gifts to offer,
and hiding your light is a sin
against the divine and humanity.

beautiful child;
this life may pain and challenge you.

you will be broken and feel so alone.
but remember, you have yourself always.
you are a part of a tribe who loves and adores you.
you are connected to the cosmos
and without you, it would be incomplete.
you are necessary and needed.

beautiful child;
others may scoff at you.
it's only because they aren't
on your wavelength.
truth be told,
they are drawn to your light,
but jealous of it too.
don't measure yourself by their sights.

beautiful child;
you are so special –
so smart, so funny, so kind.
you deserve to be loved.
and if you make a mistake
or set a boundary,
that doesn't make you
demanding and difficult.
you actually become
more worthy and stunning
because
you are respecting yourself and others,
you are taking responsibility,
you are evolving.

beautiful child;
i am madly in love with all that you are,
just as you are.

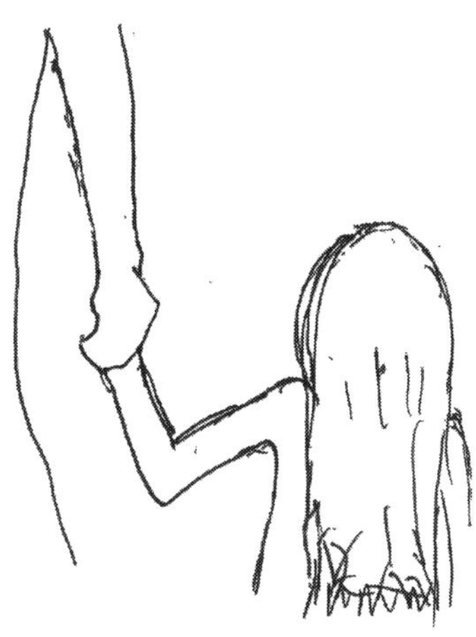

dusk

my brother's eyes – terrified
haunt me awake.

how scary when the blue ink
of madness covers his brain,
seeping into his logic
and poisoning it so quickly.
i wish i could talk away
the monster,
convince it to release
its strangle-hold on his mind.
but i sit and watch
powerless and scared,
crying a child's tears.

i pray he will forgive
my betrayal
of calling police officers for help
on this christmas eve.
we can't seem to quiet
the dragon ourselves
and all i can see are
my brother's eyes – terrified,
haunted and awake.

he is searching for the source
of the evil terrorizing him

but doesn't seem to realize
it appears from the dungeon of his brain
escaping without warning –
an impetuous fiend
gripping my brother's thoughts.

but maybe god and miracles exist,
and so i plead and beg.
if my words can manifest anything,
i hope that my brother
will be a knight again soon.
with love and the right potions,
he will be gallant in his armor.

dawn

the birds start singing
when the sun begins lightening the horizon.
and i wonder if every night
they think that life is over,
and every morning
they rejoice maddeningly
that life goes on.
i wonder if there is an exact
second in time
that they realize death
has staved off for another day.
they can fly again
with the sunshine in their feathers
and the breeze against their little faces.

does sanity and madness
work the same way?
is there a snap, click
when everything shifts impossibly
yet definitively?

i saw a twinkle in my brother's
hazel eyes that appeared like
the daylight,
and like a lark
i burst with a cacophony of sounds
when i heard his laughter.

alive for another day.
but please, i pray that night
never comes again
for him.
and if it must, can you show me
how to spark a fire to keep him
warm and hopeful?
just a little kindling and
a flicker of light
to turn dead leaves into magic.

mourning prayer

my brother asks for
the serving plate of chicken scarpariello
so he can dip his bread into the au jus,
and my mother's eyes
can't hide her joy.
having her two adult children
for dinner is her secret love.

we do it far less often
than we should,
but like a bonding after a death,
here we are
at our nightly vigil;
hopeful we are shitting shiva
and saying goodbye to that merciless dragon.

after we eat,
mom and i play cribbage.
she always wins, her pegs like stallions
nosing past turns
leaving my little elderly race horses in the dust,
confused about fifteen-twos.
hazel lies near us,
dozing off with a happy puppy belly
full of grandma's not-so-sneaked treats.
my brother will call a friend or
drift through social media.

we have gratitude together.
there is peace in this moment.

the monster
has been pushed back
into its cave for now,
lurking in the shadows.
we are hopeful that
this time
it stays there to die
a much-anticipated death.
maybe this time
we chanted correctly
and something snapped, clicked
in the universe
in the world
in his brain.

maybe this time
we spoke truth to power and
the demon will finally let us all alone.

may we keep these dinners,
these evenings, these jokes,
but lose the fiend and its poison ink
in my brother's mind.

la pietà

who told women we aren't beautiful
when we age?
we hide our wrinkled faces in shame
as though we don't somehow do
the most amazing thing
by creating life:
geniuses, poets, artists and healers.
who could not believe
god is a woman,
(and that women
are divine)?

not young and supple,
but creased with love
around the eyes.

and yet our female elders
have such visceral reactions
knowing someone outside of their families
sees them in their natural states,
sees their naked faces.

la pietà:
the tragedy of a mother
losing her child.
yet how sad that
she loses love for her own image,

as though she is not the most
perfect sight to her child.

she has loved, she has sacrificed,
she has given every part of herself;
but she wants everyone
to look elsewhere
for beauty.

survival of the fittest

even blossoms know to close
when it gets dark or cold;
i hope my heart learns
to be as smart as a flower
one day.

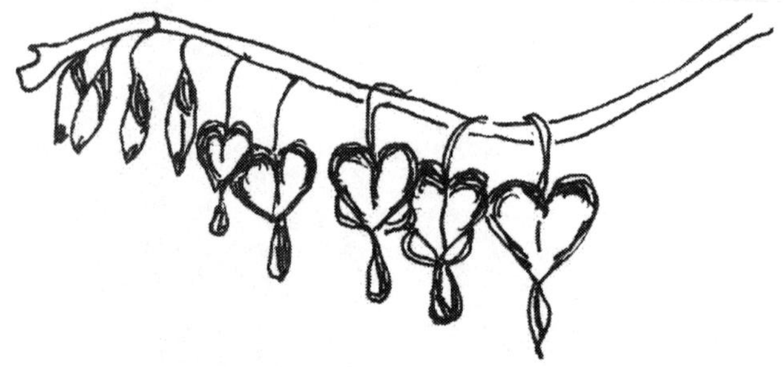

greek village rain

in the back of a beaten field
the rain hit my face,
a gift from heaven
for thirsty pastures
and tired uncles.
today yota learned to drive
and we screamed in the car
in two languages.
her father picked us small watermelons.
and after we slipped from the wet road
i jumped out to take the wheel,
but not before i picked
a solo sunflower,
tiny and magnificent.
a gift for my yia-yia.
it grew like me –
fast and proud and strong.
and after presenting my grandmother
with the heliotrope,
my cousins and i
walked between the raindrops
to the café,
where we drank frappé
and snuck cigarettes.

sinking

i was eight the first time
i swam to the floating dock
in the middle of that small lake.
maybe i was younger,
an age before life had made me
weary and afraid.
still, i had the nerves of a child
who wanted a parent's protection.

i asked my mother to watch me,
just in case.

no,
she said,
all seriousness in her voice.
no.
if you go, i won't watch.

i didn't understand.
i turned to the water
with grief in my heart.

why not encourage?
why not a desire to join your child
in conquering her fears?
why not reassure her of her strength
and cheer her on?

she challenged me instead.

but i swam anyway.

on that slippery dock,
i stood in the sun with my palms in the air
smiling at the sky at my achievement.
i tilted my face to the heavens
and then searched the beach
for pride in my mother's eyes,
but saw none.

la fortuna

of all the achievements
that made me jut my chin out in pride
and grin uncontrollably,
my cheeks becoming puffy,
my eyelashes bowing overwhelmed,
was the moment my mother saw
a picture of me worshipping
at la fortuna waterfall
and responded, “what a goddess!”

for decades i have felt unworthy.
in what moment does a girl lose her confidence?

maybe it was the day kevin begrudgingly
kissed my cheek in spin-the-bottle in eighth grade.
or was it when my priest
took me to weight-loss meetings at age eleven?

i see pictures
of that beautiful child
and recognize sadness in her eyes,
despite her deep-seated knowledge
that jesus loved everyone;
even the trans* woman
who briefly came to our services before
out pastor asked her to
kindly stop.

i never understood why god
would love me more
if i weighed a little less,
or love that trans* woman more
if she'd only be
a little less
herself.

at five years old, frankie squished my fingers
between legos and i didn't cry.
and when i was nine, tommy
kicked my skateboard,
a piece crumbled off,
and i threw him to the ground.
my brother stared amazed,
because when in my life
— then or now —
have i so boldly let someone know
that enough is enough?

i learned to set boundaries
in my twenties
but still let lovers
view them as dares
rather than walls.

what woman has not struggled,
buried her head, hunched her shoulders,
wrapped her arms around her middle,
and covered the lines of her legs?

i sometimes wonder who i would be
if i were not beaten by the world,
and raised by a woman
who was not
also beaten by the world?
she
who turned mountains into molehills
and dirt into glitter.
she
who taught me to work until
i pass out exhausted every night.
she
who carried the world on her back
so her kids could have a better life.

but we hate the shape of our chins
or the thickness of our thighs
or the unflatness of our stomachs,
so what's the point of
this fiery spirit
if it doesn't make us
pretty?

the moment my mother
called me a goddess
i realized
that's who i was
all along.

loving a narcissist

i am your lover
but you won't claim me
as your girlfriend.
i feel the mountains of silence
that exist in this tiny car.
where is my window?
and whose thighs are you thinking of
when you're not touching mine?

to whoever needs to hear it

you
you have a heart
larger than a meteor,
and it burns in the night sky
screaming and alive.

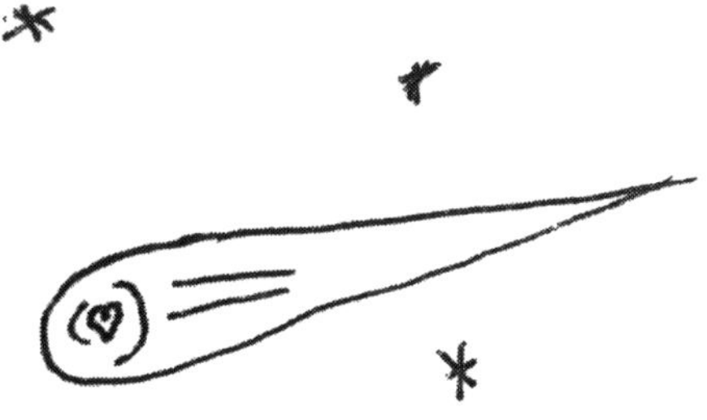

45

research shows that improving literacy
happens naturally
so i don't really teach vocabulary to my students
except in context.
and the context is all around us these days
in these
dis-united states of america.

the definition of the word of the day:
showy, shallow, worthless
the term:
trumpery.

and boy is he ever because
never
in teaching for these eleven years
have i seen such unbridled fear
in my students and their peers.
they're too afraid to ask
but they know things have shifted
in a scary direction.
victimized and vulnerable,
they know the enemy no longer lurks,
but brazenly blasts bullshit
about trying to make things great again.

but for whom?

make them great like they were for blacks
who built this country on their backs?
or for the japanese who pleaded on their knees,
"oh please don't put us away."
is this the american way?
to say to natives, who just want to thank
their mother earth
for all of the gifts she's birthed,
"we will take your mother
and put our pipeline up her.
rape her while you sit and watch
powerless
to the profit-making-machine.
why would you want your water clean,
when everything we've built
over and around you is so dirty?"

do you mean you want to make it great
and go back to the days
without trans*, lesbians or gays?
days when a woman knew her place
and if she didn't, well, just knock her in the face;
or better yet, grab her by the pussy
to make her remember her worth –
that her womb is just a room in a house
that any louse can buy.
but what it might produce?
well, she might have to obey eight guys
signing laws about her body which they despise.

do you want to go back to the good ol' days
when jews would choose
to keep to themselves,
and islam wasn't even a household word?
they stayed over there
and we ruled over here
through atomic bombs and fear.

this man is a toddler in chief.
we won't use the honorary title,
but instead, we will call him 45.
that's the term
doctor king's daughter said
we should use
to keep her parents' legacies alive.

as an educator, i am supposed to teach my kids
wrong from right
the proper way to fight,
the difference between want and need,
the ravaging nature of greed.
i try to plant the seeds of knowledge,
preach that all we need is to
communicate and cooperate
if we are really going to make this country great.

so 45, why don't you visit us and see what i see:
the great america that we want it to be.
maybe you could learn about
empathy and kindness,

self-control and minding your manners,
how to think before you speak and mean what you say,
so kellyanne doesn't have to cover your acts
trying to convince us all there are indeed
"alternative facts."

orwell warned wailing about the party
and their manipulations:
"that picture is a lie. don't believe what you see."
winston and spicer will rewrite history.
it's all fake news and doublespeak,
they tell you freedom is slavery and
ignorance is strength and
war is peace.
"what, can the devil speak true?"
says banquo to macbeth.
it was a warning: sometimes evil will hide behind
the hologram of decency; like
pretending to "drain the swamp"
with goldman sachs billionaires and ceos
and let's not forget betsy devos.

i try to convince my students
education is the key,
but everyone who got their jobs with him
had no training or integrity.
the head of the epa wants to
put big oil first and line their pockets.
the national security advisor
isn't worried about our nation's security

as much as he is with putin's plots.
and here i am trying to convince them that
true patriotism is knowledge,
and knowledge is power.
yet all they see
are poor people with degrees,
all of us holding on to a dream
that isn't really what it seems.
criminals are really calling the shots
while all the honest men and women rot.

so we will persist and resist this narcissist
while he tweets his tantrums and spouts his lies.
and one day i hope we all realize
that the people have the power
and we will capitalize on that hour
when we come to cast our votes
or walk in the streets,
telling everyone we meet
that unless we care for one another
and come together in unity

america will cease to be
what we truly know it can be.

46

an exhale
(heard round the globe)

so many of us held our breath,
believed we were suffocating
for four arduous years.

it may not fix everything,
but it’s something.

it feels like a restoration
of hope
of dignity
of honesty
of compassion
of representation
of kindness
of respect
of pride
of safety

maybe now
we can continue our journey
toward justice and equality for all.

sixth day

on the first day, god created light.

but twenty-twenty felt like darkness –
two epidemics ripped through us.

we panicked over how to avoid
contracting an illness we knew nothing about.
and even more devastating
was the other deadly disease
unfolding all over our screens:
a young female medic,
murdered while sleeping in her own bed;
a jogger, hunted down
and shot in the street;
a man suffocated by the knee of a psychopath,
while he pleaded for his life,
calling out for his mother
like a terrified toddler.

these lynchings are our country's
greatest sin and deepest shame.
and they didn't even slow
in the face of a global pandemic.

on the fourth day, god created the moon and the stars.

how glad we all were when
that ball of light dropped
ending an absurd year of the two maladies
which broke our spirits and our hearts.

this year would be different, we said.
this year we would learn from our mistakes,
this year we would heal.
this was the year for love and justice.

on the sixth day, god created people;
but on the sixth day of twenty-one, god wept.

more disturbing than our worst nightmares,
those home-grown terrorists
beat police officers to death
while waving blue lives matter flags —
was the sick irony lost on them?
they wore painted faces and rejoiced
in their destruction,
a lord of the flies shaman and
his sadistic choir.

billions of us witnessed the system protecting exactly
who it was designed to safeguard.
they knew
and we knew
those white bodies
could do whatever they pleased,
could hurt whomever they wanted,

and the whole world bore witness
to our glorious hypocrisies.

such obvious double standards, because
before that sixth day,
peaceful capitol protests showed us:
575 arrests for not wanting children and
parents separated at the border,
316 arrests for those who said black lives matter,
372 arrests for trying to stop the keystone pipeline,
147 arrests for speaking out for climate protection,
133 arrests for petitioning for lgbtq rights, and
181 arrests and forceful removals,
wheelchairs and all, for wanting continued
access to decent healthcare.

but those deranged insurrectionists
faced little opposition
from swat teams and riot gear,
tanks or cuffs.

the shaman and his hunters
walked free and proud and alive —
marching through an edifice
built by the blood of black and brown bodies,
standing on the bones and tears of those incarcerated,
simply for desiring equality for all.

on the sixth day, we wept
and god did too.

my heart

i handed you my heart the way a child
presents a drawing to her parents.

at least my mother
always had the decency
to hang it on the fridge for a while
before throwing it away.

black and white and green and oolong and fermented

today, i'm no one's cup of tea.
solitary in my steaming.

babies

i create paintings
like making a child
and you ask me to part with one.
how can i give away
my daughter's eyes,
my son's smile,
swirled against
the canvas of my heart?

life lessons

i learned shame
before i learned to speak.
i was taught my tears
were miserable things
which pierced the side of my mother.
they were prickly annoyances
that she took and piled
onto her pullulating load of things
she labeled “burdens.”
i learned to be ashamed of my wailing,
which is the only language a baby actually has.

the lesson there, of course,
is to hide your needs
and avoid crying out loudly into this world.

i learned shame
before i learned to sleep.
my infant self
already had the makings of
this anxious woman i’d become,
who thinks she can control outcomes
by keeping vigil
and worrying fate into my design.
i couldn’t trust the universe
to keep my mother safe while i dozed,
so how could i relax and fall into dreams?

the lesson there, of course,
is that tragedy is lurking around the corner
and it's your mission to fend it off.

i learned shame
before i learned to walk.
i knew there were places my body
wouldn't fit properly,
especially into the expectations of
how it should be shaped
and how much space it should take up.
i was taught to try to starve it into being a frame
upon which other people's approval
could be hung.
my own hunger for love
was just secondary in importance.
i was taught to feel guilty
if anyone touched me inappropriately
because i was somehow asking for it
by merely existing as imperfectly
and as female as i do.

the lesson there, of course, is obvious.

i learned shame
before i learned acceptance.
i learned that who i love
is something to hide,
a tragic flaw that makes me
eternally unacceptable

to my mother
and her god.
i was taught to try to make that part of me
as unnoticeable as possible.
and if, by chance, i found
a woman willing to love me,
it would not only be incomprehensible,
but something about which i should always
stay silent.

i learned shame
before i learned to imagine.
so no wonder this struggle to be
authentically proud
has felt like climbing a mountain without shoes.

but,
my feet are calloused and strong.
my toenails chipped and colorful.
my skin toughened by the sun.
my hands curled into fists.

after shame, came the new lessons:
how to find peace within me.
how to listen to my inner voice.
how to read the signs around me.
how to nurture and rejuvenate myself.
how to work toward my dreams.
how to rest and meditate and trust the process.
how to be grateful and have faith.

how to wipe away the shame
that i should never
have even learned
in the first place.

i learned truth
after i learned how
to speak
and sleep
and walk
and love.

wish list

she told me my love is like the ocean.
so why am i chasing clouds
when i deserve the whole sky?

i want to save broken birds
like somehow
their mended wings will give me flight.
i'm drawn to tortured souls.
i've always thought if i revealed to them
the beauty that exists,
they would have to love me because
i gave them god.

but what do i need?

i deserve the moonlight and the stars
when i feel dark and lost.

i want a partner, not a project.
i want to be challenged and cherished.
i want to be forgiven and adored.
i want to be touched like my body gives life.
i want to be inspired and respected.
i want to be thankful every day for synchronicity.
i want to grow together and evolve separately.

existential gasping

microcosmic anxiety —
silly when you scale it.

but against what?

in the continuum of relevancy,
what are the binaries?
god and un-creation?

i find both inside me everyday.
a baby bird.
a little war.
cute as a giggle,
sad as the only tears.

love is a drug

what's that
you say?
let me twirl
maddeningly
into the breeze.
ay me.
my tongue
searching for
your salt.
may i grow gills
god
so i can just
pass through.
writing runes
with your fingers
on my cave walls.
tonight,
let's try like hell
to make a baby.
even though
our bodies curve
in the same places.
joyous, the trying.
ay me.
my eyes
wandering down
your stone wall

at places
i can hop over
like a fox.

maybe you should have gotten over your ex-girlfriend before dating me

i want you to look at me with fire in your eyes.
instead, i see cloudy veils.
vulnerability is scary, sure.
but honestly, the way you say her name
makes this feel like an ending
rather than a beginning.

for anthony

a small detail
sends my mind into madness.
so i sit here
picking through it,
like a poor man scouring for loose change
from a hopeful spot,
cradled away in the darkness.

where oh where
has it blown?
away and down the drainpipe.

he died.
after the hardest year
he ever lived.
finding it slowly in alleyways,
glistening with sweat dripping.

these desperate lives of sullen men;
or is it
sullen lives of desperate men?

somewhere the meaning
may develop from the chaos.
until then,
i will explode on this path,
gritting my teeth.

superhero

there are not enough words
to console a grieving family.
and whether or not they believe
in heaven or an afterlife
is irrelevant,
because the loss of a child
makes it impossible to be faithful or breathe.
the air turned thick as tar
the moment we heard the words
'tumor' and 'fatal.'
everyone was in disbelief,
because six-year-olds shouldn't die.

there are not enough embraces
to nurture a grieving family.
the only touches they crave
are the little fingers of their daughter's hands,
her arms wrapped tightly around them,
her soft kisses on their cheeks.
what sort of god
allows a child to suffer
in such an agonizing way?
it's unfathomable and devastating,
because six-year-olds shouldn't die.

there are not enough photos
to soothe a grieving family.

there is only the aching knowledge
that there are no more
pictures to be taken in the future.
may she always be remembered as
that superhero in her red cape
her fist held high in delight
clenching her bubble wand,
knowing nothing of doctors
or medicines or tests
or pain, and certainly not mortality,
because six-year-olds shouldn't die.

there are not enough tears
to heal a grieving family.
these rites we perform
bring little closure for us because
they were created to honor our elders.
a little girl wearing a flowered dress
runs over to help the men in dark suits
carry her baby sister's casket,
bearing a load heavier than she can process –
all of it so twisted and heartbreaking.
no, they don't make funeral dresses
for children, and they shouldn't
make boxes that small either,
because six-years-olds shouldn't die.

she has left us, but her light remains.
but even that doesn't bring total solace,
because six-year-olds shouldn't die.

dachau

between the barrack foundations
stand trees tall as obelisks.
like flags or heroes,
they are skinny and erect,
reaching toward the heavens.

but in the grainy photographs of the camp,
they were just squat bushes ninety years ago,
crouching in the shadows
like terrified children,
witnessing horrors unspeakable.
now they are triumphant,
for evil no longer lives there.

along the perimeter, water rushes past,
trying for decades to cleanse
death from the soil.
how many tears joined this river,
flowing as far from here as one can fathom?

near the buildings where life was exterminated,
bodies turned to ash,
the silence is tangible –
somehow it becomes our breath.
we inhale souls of loved ones
and exhale grief
over the depths of human depravity.

even in the summer sun,
there is a chill here.
how could it ever be warm
in a place like this?

the other trees on the boundaries of dachau
are bowing down, their limbs heavy –
and if we cut them open, surely we would find
the red blood of our slaughtered pouring out.

even nature will never let them be forgotten.

weather report

i awake from the fog
and realize
things aren't right.

maybe it's the timing,
maybe it's just us.

either way,
my heart is a hurricane,
when it should be
a holiday.

wonderland

you poker playing sophist.
you keep your decks separate,
bidding and picking up cards,
looking for a better hand or three.

why do you make me feel like the mad hatter
when i'm really a queen?

you toss me down like a worthless hand.
yet, you'll still occasionally
lift a corner and wink at me.

fool.
i know how to play too,
but i'd rather find an alice.

i've got a land to build
so beauteous.
you'll never live in a faery tale, love,
if you spend all your time
weaving your lies.

breakfast

how did you learn to bury yourself
under the cover of your eyes?
as obvious as a pancake,
flat and dense.
i eat your words anyway,
syrup your stories so my belly ignores
what my throat chokes on.

my heart sinks
knowing that this relationship
is not some amusement park,
an exciting summer adventure.

no,
you convince me that
the fun-house mirrors
are somehow reality, undistorted.
my eyes are the problem,
my senses are wrong,
i must be crazy.

and you smirk and light your cigarette
on all this gas light you throw,
because you know my love for you
will make me question my own instincts.

deep down i understand
dating you is like
being in a rollercoaster chair
that has a safety bar
plagued with epilepsy.

one day i'll trade my entry ticket
and your sugary meals
for a cold beer on the beach,
knowing i'd rather be alone
with the waves and gulls
than in your shoddy carnival
waiting for all the red flags
to catch fire.

sacrifice

must it all be so transient?
the death of a thing
lasts longer than its life.

still

we must acknowledge
the limitless gift of itself
it gave to others,
knowing it would soon
become something else.

such wisdom,
ultimate and simple.

TAKE YOUR TIME

happy holiday

every year at this time,
it's the same sight:
christmas tree carcasses
haphazardly strewn on sidewalks,
stripped naked with their trunks in the air,
and needles littering the ground.
discarded so easily,
the season
left behind in haste.
it saddens me to see
not the usual blue recycling bins, but
the dying trees lining the curbs,
ghosts of christmas past.
but as for me,
this year i will keep my douglas fir
and her ever growing anorexic appendages.
she will dry out in the garage
and next year
she will offer up the core of herself,
which i will saw into small circles
to form homemade ornaments
that we will hang on her children.

daddy’s girl

i miss how frustrated i became
when he playfully bit my toes
to transport me back
to four and a half years old,
the last time he ever saw me.
where are my father’s eyes?
as elusive as my mother’s
but not on my side of the ocean.

soliloquy to a teacup

light so cloudy
nothing comes through.
somewhere in my tomorrows
it hit me hard and soft.
tea settle me now.

inside lives a stoic
with a conviction that all is made
how it saw fit
(and sometimes beautiful),
like encapsulated water
trying to escape into a
different sort of existence.
but dónde está mi libro?

pitter-patter poetry
lollying down rooftops.

grey day.
but inside,
the universe.
and inside that,
a smile
in which melancholy
turns us into muzicari.
productive in this lackadaisicalness.
dread not

below my fingertips
where moments become externalized.
thinkable instinct
makes my eyes blink your face away.

pocket song

i'm tired and i'm taken
if i'm not mistaken
it was in your bed
this secret desire
i'm over my head now
drowning with longing
and deep inside
i know to keep fighting
can't bottle your laughter
to take to my maker
not every wave is
called home to shore
i'm fuming with answers
to unasked questions
fed up with your bullshit
not waiting for you anymore

thimble

you took of my body
broke it and ate.
it was almost religious
this primal desire
to pin you to the bottom
of your boat
and pray between your thighs.
you made me look you
straight in the eyes,
and my god,
you were prettier
than the sun sparkling on the sound.
so this is freedom?
a baptism by fire and water
blood and wine.
my knees are bruised,
and yet, i want to kneel again,
rub them tender
against the ground
while you rub yourself tender
against my mouth.
make you scream until
you reach silence
and shake until
you reach stillness.

mystic

on a rainy day
we decide to go to the aquarium
to learn a thing or two
from our slippery friends.

the jellyfish glowing purple
with the black light remind us
to inhale
                    exhale,
as they expand
                              contract;
their entire existence
a flowing, easy movement.

the birds in the temporary sanctuary
dive-bomb us when we hold out
peanut-butter and seed covered sticks.
we shriek and pull our hoodies up,
worried it will be more than drizzle
that falls in our hair.

the penguins make the most sense,
caught between two types of creatures,
loving both water and earth.
birds that can't fly
but glide as easily as any fish.

they find one mate and
will sacrifice altruistically.
ultimately, they are more humane than
many people we've known.

we saunter slowly,
laughing at the way they play.
i love the lessons animals teach.
and i love what i'm learning about
this girl
whose fingers thread through mine.

please god,
let me fall like i would into an ocean,
becoming a mermaid.

october

i've always said
the answers are found
in nature.
at my lowest times,
i sought solace outside,
tried to make meaning,
find faith, touch divinity.
and now the girl
with eyes that look like
dark stones in a clear river
shows me other signs.
i've collected treasures:
beach glass and sand,
shells and feathers.
but she showed me the wonder
of heart-shaped rocks.
and during autumn,
the red, yellow, and orange
valentine silhouette of certain leaves;
or others with little parts worn away,
creating that negative-space
cordiform symbol of love.
and now i know i was right —
the answers are right here
in my favorite season.

fall

how fitting a description
and perfect,
her manifested totems.

i am in love.

petoskey

by the lake in michigan
we hunt for certain stones.
ancient coral broke and fossilized
and here we are centuries later
finding the remnants
like gold hunters in california.
but the worth of these rocks
is only a family decision.
to us, they are priceless.
we beam and hold up
our fists in victory
when we find the ones that are
light and dark,
able to form spider-web designs
when wet.
precious illusions;
they look like any other sea rock,
smooth and grey;
but add a little unsalted water
and there is treasure.

yesterday i walked along the beach
talking with my sister,
our deepest secrets showing.
and then i held my brother's hand
while we drunkenly
opened our hearts to one another.

i feel luckier
than i do when i find a petoskey
that i get to be a part of this family
and love a girl
more stunning than the sunset,
more rare than sea glass,
and sweeter than a mango
on a vacation morning.

soulmate

screw disney
for making girls think that
our soulmate should:

1. require us to change ourselves; and,
2. be male.

what kind of misogynistic,
heteronormative trash is that?
they rationalized losing your voice
and being trapped in a dank castle,
all in the name of "true love."
they handed that toxic mess to us
in pretty bright colors
and we consumed it eagerly.

my dog is one of my soulmates
in my little collective.
we knew each other in the
before-life
and we will be together again in the
after-life.
but the way she looks at me in
this life,
awestruck and enchanted,
makes me feel like a prince —
and i wouldn't want to change a thing
about her.

retrograde

six planets are in retrograde
right now
and we wonder why
everything is a fucking wreck.

everyone blames mercury,
that lucky bastard.
closest to the sun,
so he takes up all the glory
for this hot mess.
none of us can figure out
how to communicate,
our emotions and words are
as jumbled as space junk
flailing all over.

jupiter has us all judgey
and aloof.
uranus has us riding
a rollercoaster of feelings
and finances.
and neptune has us second-guessing
our gut instincts.

we are to breathe, patiently.

the only place i want to be
in this crazy solar system
is in bed with my dog and kitties,
the covers pulled way up,
some tea by my side.

it's not all bad news, though.

saturn's backpedal walks us
away from those toxic people
so we can commit to the right ones
during this harvest season.

and pluto,
mighty, little pluto.
the forgotten, childless
hippie aunt of our cluster.
she wants us to ameliorate and evolve,
to let go so we can grab onto
what's coming next.

all this chaos during the most
brilliant time of the year
on this silly planet.

the only way for me to survive
those roman gods traveling
in the opposite direction and
ramping up the anxiety

is simple, tested and true:

i walk outside in the forest,
follow the streams to the waterfalls.
i lie down on a boulder in the middle of nowhere
and become seven years old again.
i watch the leaves flutter down
around me,
stare at the patterns the branches
and sky make,
listen to the singing of water over rocks,
and just
be
smile
relax
and give thanks
for the goddess within me
who can outsmart those foolish
old gods any day.

CELEBRATE YOUR LIFE! GO PLAY WITH YOUR TOYS
So there we are again. You must like us! Got something to say? Email us: manicfyre@hotmail.com
or
unheardwisdom@hotmail.com
Remember to praise the goddesses in your life! PEACE + LOVE!
RANDOM THOUGHTS
"I am a work in progress
dressed in the fabric
of a world unfolding..."
Ani DiFranco

acknowledgements

i have been writing poetry since i was young. i started in middle school, continued through high school, and never stopped. as a teen, the things i wrote were mostly terrible and cheesy. i mused about longing for love, i vented about my mother, i poured out my angsty heartache at having to exist so uncomfortably in my own skin. (actually not all that different from what i write now, i just realized)

my good friend in high school, emily, convinced me that we should collect our poetry and put them into “‘zines” which we decorated with letters and pictures cut out from magazines. we quoted our favorite singers and feminists. i had never heard of ‘zines, but emily was far more worldly and much hipper than i was, so i jumped at this idea. we went to the library and made photocopies of our work and left them around the high school. we produced three or four issues and we called it ‘happy gray energy petals’ for some unknown reason. we used pseudonyms, convinced that we could hide in plain sight. i’m sure our friends knew who we were and what we were up to; and maybe they even read them, but i’m not sure if anyone else did. we gave out e-mail addresses which we created for the sole purpose (soul purpose?) of hoping others would send us their poetry and we could expand our ‘zine and become an underground sensation.

no one ever wrote to us.

but it didn't matter. we were doing something we loved and we really didn't care what anyone else thought, because what did they know anyway? right?

i had phenomenal english teachers my junior and senior years who stoked my love of reading and writing. indeed, i believe the reason i became a high school english teacher was because of rosemary purdy. of course emily and i gave our english teachers copies of our little 'zines; we wanted someone to acknowledge how exclusively cool we were. and what better humans to confirm this than our english teachers who were close to retirement?

a really interesting thing happened to me during my last year of high school: mrs. purdy entered one of my pieces into a poetry contest. i can't remember if i knew she did this or not, but somehow i won. it was the most honest thing i had written up to that point. it had nothing to do with love or anger, it was about me feeling like i didn't fit the stereotype of being a good female in this world. i wrote about unused plastic princess shoes i had received when i was five, but never wore. i gave them away to a little girl in my neighborhood when i became a teenager. the poem reflected on the fact that i never wanted to be a princess, which made me feel like i wasn't a real girl. wasn't i supposed to want to be a princess when i grew up? shouldn't i be trying to be a real girl?

the piece ended with a query about whether i could find plastic princess shoes in size 9. it wasn't a bad poem. in fact, it very purposefully called into question the gender binary training we put onto our children based merely on their sex assigned at birth. of course i didn't have that language then – i don't even think it existed as such. but as an adult, i see that this piece had substance and said something important.

i never again entered a poetry contest. it's been over twenty years, but i think i'll start sending some work out to see what the response is. i would be honored if someone wanted to print or pay me for my words. that isn't what makes art good, though; nor is it the reason anyone writes poetry in the first place. but this year, i decided to find the confidence (or stupidity) i had as a teenager and share some of my thoughts. i am hoping more people read this than read our 'zines in high school. but if not, it's okay.

anyway, i can try to tell you how nonchalant i am about all this, but i do hope something i've written resonates with you.

to all of the people who have supported me along the journey of life, i appreciate you more than i probably express.

about the author

Lisa Stamidis, author of Piera's Pilgrimage, studied literature at Boston University and earned her graduate degree in education from the University of Saint Joseph. She lives in Connecticut with her beautiful dog and two mischievous but snuggly cats. She is learning to keep plants alive. In her free time, she paints, hikes, and spends time with her loved ones. This is her first collection of poetry.

Made in the USA
Columbia, SC
09 April 2022

58739789R00062